C000263561

to Darling Lizzie, on 22nd
September 2012 — to keep you
going with all of your friends,

KEEP
CALM
AND
CUDDLE
UP

with lots of love and best wishes,
while I continue my search for
76 TROMBONES, from Beloved

For Sharon

KEEP CALM AND CUDDLE UP

GOOD ADVICE FOR THOSE IN LOVE

EBURY
PRESS

1 3 5 7 9 10 8 6 4 2

First published in 2012 by Ebury Press, an imprint of Ebury Publishing
A Random House Group company

The Random House Group Limited Reg. No. 954009

Addresses for companies within the Random House Group can be
found at www.randomhouse.co.uk

A CIP catalogue record for this book is available
from the British Library

The Random House Group Limited supports The Forest Stewardship
Council (FSC®), the leading international forest certification
organisation. Our books carrying the FSC label are printed on FSC®
certified paper. FSC is the only forest certification scheme endorsed by
the leading environmental organisations, including Greenpeace.
Our paper procurement policy can be found at
www.randomhouse.co.uk/environment

Printed in Germany by GGP Media GmbH, Pössneck

ISBN 9780091947347

To buy books by your favourite authors and register for offers visit
www.randomhouse.co.uk

WHAT THE WORLD REALLY NEEDS IS MORE LOVE AND LESS PAPER WORK.

Pearl Bailey

CONTENTS

Your cheating heart

Breaking up

The ex factor

Finding 'the one'

Love is …

Lovers' tiff

Suspicious minds

The real thing

Proposing

Like a horse and carriage

Keep the flame burning

Valentine

Birds do it, bees do it

Love is blind

Romance

INTRODUCTION

What is it about love? Songs have been composed, poems written, wars waged and lips split outside nightclubs because of it. The image of the lover is everywhere – indeed, so familiar have a few of these become that they now operate as a kind of cultural shorthand. Want to quickly show the pain of first love? Then how about a bobbysocked teenager weeping into her pillow. What about the impetuous spontaneity of youthful romance? Surely a peppy young buck, guitar strapped to his back climbing a vine to an open window.

When considering the fate of famous lovers, it's surprising that anyone goes in for it, really. Paris and Helen of Troy hooked up, only for his home town to get pillaged and burned by her jealous ex. Anthony and Cleopatra ended badly; a nasty business involving snakes. And Romeo and Juliet are enough to put anyone off for life. Every soap opera depends upon the love triangle, the thwarted desire, the forbidden love. The course of true love can never run smooth. But, and here's the odd thing, this is what we *want*. We don't actually like to see people fall happily in love and stay that way – what we prefer is for the blissful couple to be rent apart by infidelity with a randy greengrocer, or psychologically destroyed by a bitter ex who has returned to wreak havoc in paradise.

But of course, in real life, what we want is proper, true love. The search for love can lead us to some strange places, and new frontiers, but it also relies on the mundane, too. How many people met the person they love through work, for instance? Or through school or college? Or through their friends? The Venn diagrams of our lives mean that we are far more likely to meet 'the one' over the photocopier than we are when we happen to be out dragon slaying.

The newest frontier of course is the internet. Internet dating is big, big business because it works. It might seem an unnatural way to meet people, but really, is it any more of a manufactured way of meeting people than the dances and balls and formal social events of previous ages? The unique angle of internet dating, though, is potentially it allows anyone to meet *anyone*. Suddenly the pool we can fish in for a potential mate is vast. The opportunities are unlimited. But even this newest form of meeting people is still underpinned by the oldest desire – to love and be loved. St Valentine isn't likely to become the patron saint of broadband any time soon.

So enjoy this collection of lovingly selected quotes, assembled to keep the flame in your heart burning bright. In tough times when everything else becomes uncertain, there is still love. So, go on, *Keep Calm and Cuddle Up*.

ATTRACTION

EVERYONE SAYS THAT LOOKS DON'T MATTER, AGE DOESN'T MATTER, MONEY DOESN'T MATTER. BUT I NEVER MET A GIRL YET WHO HAS FALLEN IN LOVE WITH AN OLD UGLY MAN WHO'S BROKE.

Rodney Dangerfield

THE AVERAGE MAN IS MORE INTERESTED IN A WOMAN WHO IS INTERESTED IN HIM THAN HE IS IN A WOMAN WITH BEAUTIFUL LEGS.

Marlene Dietrich

THE WAY TO A WOMAN'S HEART IS THROUGH YOUR WALLET.

Frank Dane

I BELIEVE THAT IT'S BETTER TO BE LOOKED OVER THAN IT IS TO BE OVERLOOKED.

Mae West

**SCIENTISTS NOW
BELIEVE THAT
THE PRIMARY
BIOLOGICAL
FUNCTION OF
BREASTS IS TO
MAKE MALES
STUPID.**

Dave Barry

A CLEVER, UGLY MAN EVERY NOW AND THEN IS SUCCESSFUL WITH THE LADIES, BUT A HANDSOME FOOL IS IRRESISTIBLE.

William Makepeace Thackeray

LUST FADES, SO YOU'D BETTER BE WITH SOMEONE WHO CAN STAND YOU.

Alan Zweibel

FLIRTING

FLIRTATION: ATTENTION WITHOUT INTENTION.

Paul Blouet

TO AVOID MISTAKES AND REGRETS, ALWAYS CONSULT YOUR WIFE BEFORE ENGAGING IN A FLIRTATION.

E W Howe

A BEAUTY IS A WOMAN YOU NOTICE; A CHARMER IS ONE WHO NOTICES YOU.

Adlai Stevenson II

WHY DOES A
MAN TAKE IT FOR
GRANTED THAT A
GIRL WHO FLIRTS
WITH HIM WANTS HIM
TO KISS HER – WHEN,
NINE TIMES OUT
OF TEN, SHE ONLY
WANTS HIM TO WANT
TO KISS HER?

Helen Rowland

FLIRTING IS THE SIN OF THE VIRTUOUS AND THE VIRTUE OF THE SINFUL.

Paul Bourget

SEDUCTION

A WOMAN'S CHASTITY CONSISTS, LIKE AN ONION, OF A SERIES OF COATS.

Nathaniel Hawthorne

THE RESISTANCE OF A WOMAN TO A MAN'S ADVANCES IS NOT ALWAYS A SIGN OF VIRTUE. SOMETIMES IT'S JUST A SIGN OF EXPERIENCE.

Ninon de Lenclos

THE ART OF LOVE ...
IS LARGELY THE ART
OF PERSISTENCE.

Albert Ellis

A GENTLEMAN
IS SIMPLY A
PATIENT WOLF.

Lana Turner

A GENTLEMAN
DOESN'T POUNCE,
HE GLIDES.

Quentin Crisp

DATING

DATING IS PRESSURE AND TENSION. WHAT IS A DATE, REALLY, BUT A JOB INTERVIEW THAT LASTS ALL NIGHT?

Jerry Seinfeld

ODDS ON MEETING A
SINGLE MAN: 1 IN 23;
A CUTE, SINGLE MAN:
1 IN 429; A CUTE,
SINGLE, SMART MAN:
1 IN 3,245,873; WHEN
YOU LOOK YOUR
BEST: 1 IN A BILLION.

Lorna Adler

WATCHING YOUR
DAUGHTER BEING
COLLECTED BY HER
DATE FEELS LIKE
HANDING OVER A
MILLION DOLLAR
STRADIVARIUS
TO A GORILLA.

Jim Bishop

EMPLOYEES MAKE THE BEST DATES. YOU DON'T HAVE TO PICK THEM UP AND THEY'RE ALWAYS TAX-DEDUCTIBLE.

Andy Warhol

MY FATHER TOLD
ME ALL ABOUT THE
BIRDS AND THE BEES,
THE LIAR – I WENT
STEADY WITH A
WOODPECKER TILL
I WAS TWENTY-ONE.

Bob Hope

(COMPUTER DATING) IT'S TERRIFIC IF YOU'RE A COMPUTER.

Rita Mae Brown

**A MAN CAN
SLEEP AROUND NO
QUESTIONS ASKED,
BUT IF A WOMAN
MAKES 19 OR 20
MISTAKES, SHE'S
A TRAMP.**

Joan Rivers

UNREQUITED LOVE

LET NO ONE WHO LOVES BE CALLED UNHAPPY. EVEN LOVE UNRETURNED HAS ITS RAINBOW.

J M Barrie

NOTHING TAKES THE TASTE OUT OF PEANUT BUTTER QUITE LIKE UNREQUITED LOVE.

Charlie Brown

PERHAPS A GREAT LOVE IS NEVER RETURNED.

Dag Hammarskjöld

SYMPTOMS
OF LOVE

LOVE IS LIKE AN HOURGLASS, WITH THE HEART FILLING UP AS THE BRAIN EMPTIES.

Jules Renard

LOVE IS LIKE THE MEASLES, ALL THE WORSE WHEN IT COMES LATE.

Mary Roberts Rinehart

ROMANTIC LOVE IS
MENTAL ILLNESS. BUT
IT'S A PLEASURABLE
ONE. IT'S A DRUG. IT
DISTORTS REALITY,
AND THAT'S THE POINT
OF IT. IT WOULD BE
IMPOSSIBLE TO FALL IN
LOVE WITH SOMEONE
THAT YOU REALLY SAW.

Fran Lebowitz

LOVE – A WILDLY
MISUNDERSTOOD
ALTHOUGH HIGHLY
DESIRABLE MALFUNCTION
OF THE HEART WHICH
WEAKENS THE BRAIN,
CAUSES EYES TO
SPARKLE, CHEEKS TO
GLOW, BLOOD PRESSURE
TO RISE AND THE LIPS
TO PUCKER.

Anon

FIRST LOVE

EVERY MAN IS
THOROUGHLY HAPPY
TWICE IN HIS LIFE:
JUST AFTER HE HAS
MET HIS FIRST LOVE,
AND JUST AFTER
HE HAS LEFT HIS
LAST ONE.

H L Mencken

IT IS EASIER TO GUARD A SACK FULL OF FLEAS THAN A GIRL IN LOVE.

Yiddish proverb

ONE IS VERY CRAZY
WHEN IN LOVE.

Freud

MEN ALWAYS WANT
TO BE A WOMAN'S
FIRST LOVE. WOMEN
HAVE A MORE
SUBTLE INSTINCT:
WHAT THEY LIKE
IS TO BE A MAN'S
LAST ROMANCE.

Oscar Wilde

BOYS WILL BE BOYS. AND EVEN THAT WOULDN'T MATTER IF ONLY WE COULD PREVENT GIRLS FROM BEING GIRLS.

Anthony Hawkins

LOVE MAKES THE TIME PASS. TIME MAKES LOVE PASS.

Euripides

HOW ON EARTH ARE YOU EVER GOING TO EXPLAIN IN TERMS OF CHEMISTRY AND PHYSICS SO IMPORTANT A BIOLOGICAL PHENOMENON AS FIRST LOVE?

Einstein

KISSES AND CUDDLES

ALWAYS REMEMBER THIS: 'A KISS WILL NEVER MISS, AND AFTER MANY KISSES A MISS BECOMES A MISSES'.

John Lennon

A KISS IS A LOVELY
TRICK DESIGNED BY
NATURE TO STOP
SPEECH WHEN
WORDS BECOME
SUPERFLUOUS.

Ingrid Bergman

IF YOU ARE EVER
IN DOUBT AS TO
WHETHER TO KISS
A PRETTY GIRL,
ALWAYS GIVE HER
THE BENEFIT OF
THE DOUBT.

Thomas Carlyle

A KISS CAN BE A COMMA, A QUESTION MARK OR AN EXCLAMATION POINT. THAT'S BASIC SPELLING THAT EVERY WOMAN OUGHT TO KNOW.

Mistinguett

IT TAKES A LOT OF EXPERIENCE FOR A GIRL TO KISS LIKE A BEGINNER.

Ladies Home Journal, 1948

YOUR
CHEATING
HEART

IF YOU MARRY A MAN WHO CHEATS ON HIS WIFE, YOU'LL BE MARRIED TO A MAN WHO CHEATS ON HIS WIFE.

Ann Landers

A CODE
OF HONOUR:
NEVER APPROACH
A FRIEND'S
GIRLFRIEND
OR WIFE WITH
MISCHIEF AS YOUR
GOAL. THERE ARE
JUST TOO MANY
WOMEN IN THE
WORLD TO JUSTIFY

THAT SORT OF DISHONOURABLE BEHAVIOUR. UNLESS SHE'S REALLY ATTRACTIVE.

Bruce Jay Friedman

IT IS BETTER TO BE UNFAITHFUL THAN TO BE FAITHFUL WITHOUT WANTING TO BE.

Brigitte Bardot

**MY ATTITUDE
TOWARD MEN WHO
MESS AROUND IS
SIMPLE: IF YOU FIND
'EM, KILL 'EM.**

Loretta Lynn

NO LOVER, IF HE BE OF GOOD FAITH, AND SINCERE, WILL DENY HE WOULD PREFER TO SEE HIS MISTRESS DEAD THAN UNFAITHFUL.

Marquis de Sade

EVERY MAN NEEDS TWO WOMEN: A QUIET HOME-MAKER, AND A THRILLING NYMPH.

Iris Murdoch

ALL IS FAIR IN
LOVE AND WAR.

Edward Smedley

BREAKING
UP

DON'T CRY FOR A MAN WHO'S LEFT YOU, THE NEXT ONE MAY FALL FOR YOUR SMILE.

Mae West

DON'T CRY
BECAUSE IT'S OVER.
SMILE BECAUSE IT
HAPPENED.

Dr Seuss

POSSIBLY THE WORST
BREAK UP LINE EVER:
IT'S NOT ME, IT'S YOU.

Anon

DON'T WASTE TIME TRYING TO BREAK A MAN'S HEART; BE SATISFIED IF YOU CAN JUST MANAGE TO CHIP IT IN A BRAND NEW PLACE.

Helen Rowland

THE HEART WAS
MADE TO BE BROKEN.

Oscar Wilde

IT IS FOOLISH TO TEAR ONE'S HAIR IN GRIEF, AS THOUGH SORROW WOULD BE MADE LESS BY BALDNESS.

Cicero

THE HOTTEST LOVE HAS THE COLDEST END.

Socrates

FRIENDSHIP IS CERTAINLY THE FINEST BALM FOR THE PANGS OF DISAPPOINTED LOVE.

Jane Austen

IN THE ARITHMETIC
OF LOVE, ONE PLUS
ONE EQUALS
EVERYTHING, AND
TWO MINUS ONE
EQUALS NOTHING.

Mignon McLaughlin

THE EX
FACTOR

SCRATCH A LOVER,
AND FIND A FOE.

Dorothy Parker

A WOMAN'S DESIRE FOR REVENGE OUTLASTS ALL HER OTHER EMOTIONS.

Cyril Connolly

LOOKING GOOD IS
THE BEST REVENGE.

Ivana Trump

IS THERE A CURE FOR
A BROKEN HEART?
ONLY TIME CAN HEAL
YOUR BROKEN
HEART, JUST AS
TIME CAN HEAL HIS
BROKEN ARMS
AND LEGS.

Miss Piggy

FINDING
'THE ONE'

WOMEN DESIRE SIX THINGS: THEY WANT THEIR HUSBANDS TO BE BRAVE, WISE, RICH, GENEROUS, OBEDIENT TO WIFE, AND LIVELY IN BED.

Chaucer

WHEN YOU LOVE SOMEONE ALL YOUR SAVED-UP WISHES START COMING OUT.

Elizabeth Bowen

BETTER TO HAVE LOVED A SHORT MAN THAN NEVER TO HAVE LOVED A TALL.

David Chambless

PUT YOUR HAND
ON A STOVE FOR
A MINUTE AND IT
SEEMS LIKE AN HOUR.
SIT WITH THAT
SPECIAL GIRL FOR AN
HOUR AND IT SEEMS
LIKE A MINUTE.
THAT'S RELATIVITY.

Einstein

LOVE IS ...

LOVE IS SAYING
'I FEEL DIFFERENTLY'
INSTEAD OF
'YOU'RE WRONG'.

Anon

THREE GRAND ESSENTIALS TO HAPPINESS IN THIS LIFE ARE SOMETHING TO DO, SOMETHING TO LOVE, AND SOMETHING TO HOPE FOR.

Joseph Addison

TRUE LOVE IS LIKE GHOSTS, WHICH EVERYBODY TALKS ABOUT AND FEW HAVE SEEN.

François, Duc de La Rochefoucauld

ONE WORD FREES US OF ALL THE WEIGHT AND PAIN OF LIFE: THAT WORD IS LOVE.

Sophocles

LET YOUR LOVE
BE LIKE THE MISTY
RAINS, COMING
SOFTLY, BUT
FLOODING
THE RIVER.

Proverb

LOVE IS A FIRE.
BUT WHETHER IT IS
GOING TO WARM
YOUR HEARTH OR
BURN DOWN YOUR
HOUSE, YOU CAN
NEVER TELL.

Joan Crawford

LOVE IS AN OCEAN OF EMOTIONS ENTIRELY SURROUNDED BY EXPENSES.

Lord Dewar

LOVE IS METAPHYSICAL GRAVITY.

R Buckminster Fuller

LOVERS'
TIFF

SILENCE IS ONE OF THE HARDEST ARGUMENTS TO REFUTE.

Josh Billings

NEVER GO TO
BED MAD. STAY UP
AND FIGHT.

Phyllis Diller

ONCE A WOMAN HAS FORGIVEN HER MAN, SHE MUST NOT REHEAT HIS SINS FOR BREAKFAST.

Marlene Dietrich

THE COURSE OF TRUE LOVE NEVER DID RUN SMOOTH.

Shakespeare

SUSPICIOUS
MINDS

WHEN A HUSBAND BRINGS HIS WIFE FLOWERS FOR NO REASON, THERE'S A REASON.

Molly McGee

JEALOUSY IS
ALL THE FUN YOU
THINK THEY HAD.

Erica Jong

MEN ARE ONLY AS LOYAL AS THEIR OPTIONS.

Bill Maher

THE REAL
THING

**ANYONE CAN BE
PASSIONATE, BUT IT
TAKES REAL LOVERS
TO BE SILLY.**

Rose Franken

TRUE LOVE IS LIKE A PAIR OF SOCKS: YOU GOTTA HAVE TWO AND THEY'VE GOTTA MATCH.

Anon

MOST PEOPLE WOULD RATHER GIVE THAN GET AFFECTION.

Aristotle

WE DON'T BELIEVE IN RHEUMATISM AND TRUE LOVE UNTIL AFTER THE FIRST ATTACK.

Marie von Ebner-Eschenbach

IF LOVE IS THE ANSWER, COULD YOU PLEASE REPHRASE THE QUESTION?

Lily Tomlin

IN A GREAT
ROMANCE, EACH
PERSON BASICALLY
PLAYS A PART
THAT THE OTHER
REALLY LIKES.

Elizabeth Ashley

IN OUR LIFE THERE IS
A SINGLE COLOUR,
AS ON AN ARTIST'S
PALETTE, WHICH
PROVIDES THE
MEANING OF LIFE
AND ART. IT IS THE
COLOUR OF LOVE.

Marc Chagall

LOVE WON'T BE
TAMPERED WITH,
LOVE WON'T GO
AWAY. PUSH IT TO
ONE SIDE AND
IT CREEPS TO
THE OTHER.

Louise Erdich

PROPOSING

THE SUREST WAY TO HIT A WOMAN'S HEART IS TO TAKE AIM KNEELING.

Douglas William Jerrold

MAN
PROPOSES,
WOMAN
FORECLOSES.

Minna Antrim

LIKE A
HORSE AND
CARRIAGE

BRIDE. A WOMAN WITH A FINE PROSPECT OF HAPPINESS BEHIND HER.

Ambrose Bierce

MARRIAGE IS MORE THAN FOUR BARE LEGS IN A BED.

Hoshang N Akhtar

NEVER MARRY A MAN WHO HATES HIS MOTHER, BECAUSE HE'LL END UP HATING YOU.

Jill Bennett

BEFORE MARRIAGE
A MAN YEARNS
FOR A WOMAN.
AFTERWARD THE
'Y' IS SILENT.

W A Clarke

WHATEVER YOU MAY LOOK LIKE, MARRY A MAN YOUR OWN AGE – AS YOUR BEAUTY FADES, SO WILL HIS EYESIGHT.

Phyllis Diller

HAPPINESS IN MARRIAGE IS ENTIRELY A MATTER OF CHANCE.

Jane Austen

I THINK MEN WHO
HAVE A PIERCED
EAR ARE BETTER
PREPARED FOR
MARRIAGE. THEY'VE
EXPERIENCED PAIN
AND BOUGHT
JEWELRY.

Rita Rudner

KEEP THE
FLAME
BURNING

ONE SHOULD ALWAYS BE IN LOVE. THAT IS THE REASON ONE SHOULD NEVER MARRY.

Oscar Wilde

A SLIGHT TOUCH OF FRIENDLY MALICE AND AMUSEMENT TOWARDS THOSE WE LOVE KEEPS OUR AFFECTIONS FOR THEM FROM TURNING FLAT.

Logan Pearsall Smith

THERE ARE TWO WAYS TO HANDLE A WOMAN, AND NOBODY KNOWS EITHER OF THEM.

Kin Hubbard

DON'T MISTAKE PLEASURE FOR HAPPINESS. THEY ARE A DIFFERENT BREED OF DOG.

Josh Billings

A SENTIMENTAL PERSON THINKS THINGS WILL LAST; A ROMANTIC PERSON HOPES AGAINST HOPE THAT THEY WON'T.

F Scott Fitzgerald

MEN ARE FROM EARTH. WOMEN ARE FROM EARTH. DEAL WITH IT.

George Carlin

VALENTINE

I DON'T UNDERSTAND
WHY CUPID WAS
CHOSEN TO REPRESENT
VALENTINE'S DAY.
WHEN I THINK ABOUT
ROMANCE, THE LAST
THING ON MY MIND IS
A SHORT, CHUBBY
TODDLER COMING AT
ME WITH A WEAPON.

Anon

BIRDS DO IT,
BEES DO IT ...

**BISEXUALITY
IMMEDIATELY
DOUBLES YOUR
CHANCES FOR
A DATE ON
SATURDAY NIGHT.**

Woody Allen

ANY WOMAN WHO
THINKS THE WAY TO
A MAN'S HEART IS
THROUGH HIS
STOMACH IS AIMING
ABOUT 10 INCHES
TOO HIGH.

Adrienne E Gusoff

LOVE IS NOT THE DYING MOAN OF A DISTANT VIOLIN – IT'S THE TRIUMPHANT TWANG OF A BEDSPRING.

S J Perelman

LOVE IS THE SAME AS LIKE EXCEPT YOU FEEL SEXIER.

Judith Viorst

WHOEVER NAMED IT NECKING IS A POOR JUDGE OF ANATOMY.

Groucho Marx

LOVE IS
BLIND

A MAN IN LOVE
MISTAKES A PIMPLE
FOR A DIMPLE.

Japanese proverb

LOVE MAY BE BLIND, BUT IT CAN SURE FIND ITS WAY AROUND IN THE DARK!

Anon

THE ADVANTAGE OF LOVE AT FIRST SIGHT IS THAT IT DELAYS A SECOND SIGHT.

Natalie Clifford Barney

**LOVE IS THE
DELIGHTFUL
INTERVAL BETWEEN
MEETING A
BEAUTIFUL GIRL
AND DISCOVERING
THAT SHE LOOKS
LIKE A HADDOCK.**

John Barrymore

**SOME PEOPLE ARE
BETTER IMAGINED IN
ONE'S BED THAN
FOUND THERE IN
THE MORNING.**

P J O'Rourke

BEAUTY IS ALL VERY WELL AT FIRST SIGHT; BUT WHO EVER LOOKS AT IT WHEN IT HAS BEEN IN THE HOUSE THREE DAYS?

George Bernard Shaw

ROMANCE

ROMANCE IS A LOVE AFFAIR IN OTHER THAN DOMESTIC SURROUNDINGS.

Sir Walter Raleigh

ROMANCE HAS BEEN ELEGANTLY DEFINED AS THE OFFSPRING OF FICTION AND LOVE.

Benjamin Disraeli

IN ORDER TO LOVE SIMPLY, IT IS NECESSARY TO KNOW HOW TO SHOW LOVE.

Dostoyevsky

NOBODY HAS EVER MEASURED, EVEN POETS, HOW MUCH A HEART CAN HOLD.

Zelda Fitzgerald

LOVE DOESN'T MAKE THE WORLD GO ROUND, LOVE IS WHAT MAKES THE RIDE WORTHWHILE.

Franklin P Jones

COME LIVE IN MY HEART, AND PAY NO RENT.

Samuel Lover

MORE HELP
IS AT HAND...